THE
BALLANTINE
REFERENCE
LIBRARY

NEW WORDS
DICTIONARY

THE
BALLANTINE
REFERENCE
LIBRARY

NEW WORDS DICTIONARY

HAROLD LEMAY, SID LERNER, AND MARIAN TAYLOR

BALLANTINE BOOKS • NEW YORK

Library of Congress Catalog Card Number: 85-90747

ISBN 0-345-32461-7

Manufactured in the United States of America

First Edition: October 1985

PREFACE

New words are now entering the English language at an ever-increasing rate. Those of us who compile large dictionaries sift through tens of thousands of potential new entries for each new edition. In the rapid ebb and flow of language, standard dictionaries cannot list all the words and expressions in frequent use at any one moment: to do so would require that a new dictionary be printed every week and that all the unimportant words and expressions that were coined to live for a day or a few weeks would need to be listed.

Even though the best standard dictionaries, such as the *Random House College Dictionary*, may be updated every two years, there is a necessary time lag in collecting and verifying new words and checking their exact pronunciations, meanings, uses, and etymologies, and then editing, proofreading, printing, and binding a large book. In addition, there are many ephemeral words, short-lived catch phrases, slogans, and terms, in the news for a few days or weeks because they are attached to one political speech or news item, that are only of brief, topical interest and are thus never entered in standard dictionaries. This leaves us with flurries of words and phrases scattered throughout our newspapers and magazines, rolling out of our radios and television sets, swirling through the air of our homes, workplaces, schools, and streets which are not yet recorded or may never need be recorded in any authoritative dictionary.

Thus, there is a need for a small, informal book of new words, one that can be produced quickly and without consideration of the criteria and standards of authoritative dictionaries, a book for those who are interested in the latest words and expressions, whether or not these prove to be important or unimportant, long-lasting or just passing. This book attempts to fill that need. It is not meant to be a complete or even a precise coverage of new words and expressions but is for those who need or want to have a good sampling of them even before they can be pinned down as to importance or exact use. The authors of this book do not pretend to be professional lexicographers and do not attempt to be arbiters in the world of today's neologisms. They do not promise that their work is based on the vast citation files, a staff of experienced dictionary editors and consultants, or the years of research, checking, and painstaking editing needed to create major dictionaries. They do, however, promise to be alert, to serve as part of an early-warning system of new terms that may become important in the language, and to attempt informal definitions from the first, imprecise evidence while the terms may still be emerging and not fully formed.

The New Words Dictionary promises only one thing: to be interesting to all those who want to keep abreast—right now—of our constantly changing language. It will be useful to all who want to know at least the preliminary meaning of current new terms, whether or not all these terms will be needed tomorrow as well as today, useful to those who want advance warning of words that may enter our standard dictionaries after they have proved their usefulness and been pinned down more exactly.

This, then, is an informal, unscientific sampling of important, or often merely interesting, new words and expressions. It will make every reader more aware of our ever-changing vocabulary, of the fluctuation of words in modern life. It will also make every reader more aware of, and better able to talk and write about, current events, trends, and fads, better able to keep up with today's world by becoming aware of today's words.

Stuart Flexner

INTRODUCTION

This book is an eclectic assemblage of new words currently used by people of all ages, in all professions, and at all economic levels. As we go to press, few of these words—with their up-to-the-minute meanings—appear in any of the superb college dictionaries now available. We make no claim to listing *all* the not-yet-dictionaried words in use; we do claim that sooner or later you will run into many of these words in everday contexts.

Some of the words in this book will take root in the language and will appear in upcoming major dictionaries. Some won't. Some of them will be used over and over for a few weeks or months and will then pass, unmourned, into the limbo of yesterday's *lingo*. Even if a word has a short life, however, it's important to know what it means while it is appearing in headlines and talk shows. The words and phrases in this book are in frequent use *now*. Not to understand them puts us at risk of not fully understanding the world we live in.

In gathering words for this book, we have reviewed newspapers, magazines, books, pamphlets, labels, catalogues. We have listened to radio and television, to conversations in trains, at sports arenas, rock concerts, computer conventions. We have consulted experts in many fields. Our hardest job was not finding and defining new words; it was finding, defining, and *not* including certain new words. The slang words we have chosen, for example, we encountered in places like *The Wall Street Journal* and TV's *60 Minutes*, as well as on the street. There are, of course, hundreds of others, many of which, if they survive long enough to be recorded, will find homes in future compilations of colloquialisms. *Dweeb* and *happy camper* tempted us, but we drew the line after entering such frequently used words as *airhead, nose candy*, and *dorky*.

Other words absent from these pages are most of those in the "inside" lexicons of special or technical fields. Take medicine: We accepted *gomer* and *box*, but left out a book's worth of expressions used by doctors in sentences like this one from a *New York Times* column by Perri Klass: "Mrs. Tolstoy is your basic LOL in NAD, admitted for a soft ruleout MI." (Translation: Mrs. T. is a Little Old Lady in No Apparent Distress who is in the hospital to make sure she has not had a heart attack [rule out myocardial infarction].)

Or, in the computer world, for instance, we assumed that people who need to know the new words spawned daily either already know them or will use one of the many techno-specific books about them, and therefore we have not included many. Exceptions are such terms as *hacker, computerist, user-friendly*, and *electronic cottage*, which have migrated from the narrow streams of their conception to the mainstream of popular language.

Nor have we included much prison language: rough, salty, sometimes dazzling stuff, but most of it—for obvious reasons—not often printed in general-circulation publications and not in widespread use. You will, however, note a few prison-originated words that are regularly heard on the sunny side of the walls, such as *bit* and *joint*. Another float of words and expressions spring from government and military sources. Particularly hard to reject were newspeak phrases like "terminate with extreme prejudice" for *kill*, "permanent prehostility" for *peacetime*, "predawn vertical insertion" for *early-morning airborne invasion*, and "controlled flight into terrain" for *plane crash*.

College students have always been a rich source for new language, and there are many dorm-born words here. Others, such as the mellifluous *practutiation* (the creation of external motion by such internal motion as heartbeats), a popular term-paper coinage at Ithaca College, will have to last at least a whole semester before they find their places among our *New Words*.

The words that do, at last, appear in this book are likely to pop up anywhere. Readers will already know what some of them mean. We guarantee that none of you will know them all. We have not *decided* what these words mean; we are merely reporting that they are currently used in certain ways to mean certain specific things. Some readers may dispute our definitions or have additional meanings for these words. We'd like to hear from you. In the next edition of *The New Words Dictionary*, we'll use appropriate additions and suggestions you send us. (For more information, see the back of this book.)

ACKNOWLEDGMENTS

The authors are grateful for advice and contributions from Michael Agnes; Leslie Bargnesi; Larry Earle Bone; Harold I. Drucker; Daniel Flanagan; Mark Fortgang; Daniel Gardner; Froma Joselow; Helaine Lerner; Stanley Nass; Amanda Naughton; Emily, Josh, and Adam Rechnitz; Leo Stanger; Blakelock Taylor, Creed Taylor Jr., and John Wendes.

acyclovir uh-SIK-luh-vur *(noun)*
An orally administered drug approved in 1985 by the Food and Drug Administration for the treatment of genital herpes, a sexually transmitted disease that affects between 5 million and 20 million Americans. While acyclovir has been demonstrated as effective in reducing the recurrence and severity of herpes attacks, it does not cure the disease.

Ada AY-duh *(noun)*
A computer language used principally by the U.S. Defense Department. It was named for Lord Byron's daughter, Augusta Ada, who with British mathematician Charles Babbage developed a computer design in 1834 that foreshadowed much of this century's computer research.

advertorial *(noun)*
A supplement or a feature section in a newspaper or magazine composed of both display advertising and editorial material that promotes the products, services, or organizations being advertised and that clearly resembles the publication's regular editorial pages.

afterburst *(noun)*
The phenomenon presumed to follow a nuclear war, in which radioactivity would be released into the earth's atmosphere, water, and soil, as well as into the tissues of all animal and plant life, there to remain indefinitely.

aging gene *(noun)*
Term used by medical researchers for the as-yet-unidentified substance that creates the signs of old age in mammals: gray hair, wrinkles, brittle bones, menopause, etc.

agrigenetics *(noun)*
Biotechnical research in plant breeding; the attempt to control plant evolution by genetic manipulation and gene splicing to provide desirable new varieties, such as a (still-experimental) strain of wheat with the soybean's capability of fertilizing its roots with airborne nitrogen. Agrigeneticists have produced such new agricultural items as a redder, less watery commercial tomato and disease-resistant sugar cane.

aircraft carrier *(noun)*
A star basketball center who excels at handling the ball, making baskets, and playing defense.

airhead *(noun)*
A person with very little sense. Such an individual may also be called a "breeze brain" or "ditz" and may be said to be "very loosely wrapped" or to "have an elevator that doesn't reach the top floor." "What joy Americans take in calling each other stupid, and how restlessly we grope for new ways to do so. The latest variation is 'airhead,'" commented *The New York Times* in early 1985.

allophone *(noun)*
Any person who does not speak French, particularly in

Canada, where the use of French, especially in government communications, is an important political issue.

ambisonic am-buh-SON-ik *(adjective)*
A form of high-fidelity sound reproduction that, by electronically simulating the directional attributes of the sound waves it disseminates, gives the listener the impression he is in the center of a group of instruments or singers. Ambisonic music is sometimes called "surround sound."

Ames test *(noun)*
A method of testing for carcinogens through the study of their mutation-causing effects on bacteria. The ability to produce mutations often indicates a similar ability to produce cancer.

animal *(noun)*
Politicians' and journalists' term for a reporter, technician, or photographer who accompanies candidates on flying campaign trips. *Animals* are a shade lower in the hierarchy of the trade than the politicians and top-level newspeople whom they often follow in a *zoo plane*, a second, far less luxurious aircraft than that allotted their colleagues.

animal rights movement *(noun)*
A burgeoning worldwide crusade that teaches that the pleasure or pain felt by animals is as important as the pleasure or pain felt by human beings. Animal rights activists have launched recent, strenuous campaigns against laboratory experimentation on animals, seal hunting, and *factory farming*.

antichoice *(adjective)*
Opposed to the concept that pregnant women should be free to choose whether or not to have an abortion.

anti-lifer *(noun)*
Disparaging term for one who favors abortion on demand; opposite of *pro-lifer*.

Anzus AN-zus *(noun)*
Acronym for Australia–New Zealand–United States, a mutual-defense alliance of the three nations.

arb *(noun)*
Abbreviation for arbitrageur, or risk arbitrageur, a Wall Street trader who seeks profits from buying and quickly selling stocks in companies that announce merger plans.

aristology *(noun)*
"The science of dining or the art of eating well," according to food authority Craig Claiborne, who quotes an essay on aristology asserting that "the number of guests at a meal should not exceed eight and ideally there should be only six so that the conversation may be general."

Arkie AR-kee *(noun)*
The computer-games industry's equivalent of an Oscar. Arkie winners are selected by a reader poll conducted by *Electronic Games* magazine.

aromatherapy *(noun)*
A cosmetic treatment consisting of aromatic facials with floral and herbal masks blended in accordance with the client's skin type. Aromatherapy, said *Vogue* magazine, "is aimed at energizing or calming the skin *and* the spirits."

artificial gill *(noun)*
An experimental system for extracting oxygen from sea-water; its future application is expected to be in making available unlimited oxygen supplies for divers and submarines.

artificial intelligence *(noun)*
Quality possessed by a computer programmed with special information that allows it to respond to questions and situations in a human way. (See also *intelligent*.)

artsport *(noun)*
A form of modern dance that uses movements usually associated with athletics or gymnastics.

Atari Democrat *(noun)*
An epithet adapted from the trademarked Atari computer to describe a new generation of young, liberal politicians who aim at applying high-technology solutions to current problems.

ATM *(noun)*
Abbreviation for automatic teller machine, a *plastic money*-activated device that permits bank customers to deposit or withdraw funds around the clock.

baby boomer *(noun)*
A person born between 1946 and 1964, the period in American history with the highest birthrate. Boomers may also be *yuppies* or *yumpies*.

Bambi syndrome *(noun)*
The condition resulting when wild animals, usually those in national parks, are treated by tourists as though they were Disney-style pets, with the result that the animals become dangerously "friendly." Some authorities attribute an increase in bear attacks to this syndrome.

bareboat *(noun)*
A boat offered for charter that is supplied with equipment and provisions but not with a crew.

bargaining chip *(noun)*
One of the items used by either side to gain advantage when negotiating a contract or agreement.

barn burner *(noun)*
An exciting, emotion-provoking event, often a sermon or political address. *The New York Times* quoted an observer at the 1984 Democratic Convention who called the keynote speech of New York Governor Mario Cuomo "an old-time, flat-out barn burner."

BBS *(noun)*
(See *bulletin board system*.)

bicoastal *(adjective)*
Pertaining to an individual who lives and works on both the Atlantic and Pacific coasts of the United States and who is, therefore, frequently found aboard transcontinental flights; a bicoastal person is usually assumed to be sophisticated and a member of the "jet-set."

big-ticket *(adjective)*
Expensive. "Orders to U.S. factories for big-ticket durable goods plunged 4.3 percent in December" (Hartford *Courant*). "A big-ticket military: Are America's defenses billions of dollars better off?" (*Newsweek* headline).

biobelt *(noun)*
A device worn by an astronaut around the waist to record and transmit data on his physiological processes to mission control.

bioreactor *(noun)*
A living cell culture genetically engineered to produce materials useful for research in biology, medicine, and industrial processes.

birth parent *(noun)*
A biological, as opposed to adoptive, mother or father; used

with increasing frequency in referring to the searches by
adoptees for their "natural" parents.

blackened fish *(noun)*
A popular item in Cajun cuisine, consisting of pieces of
fish that have been charred on a very hot griddle or skillet
after being dipped in a mixture that includes red and white
pepper and garlic. (See also *Cajun popcorn*.)

black spot *(noun)*
A black-populated village in South Africa that is isolated
within a larger white community. One of the stated goals
of the nation's apartheid policy is to eliminate such areas
by moving their residents into the "homelands" that are
reserved for blacks and that constitute 14 percent of South
Africa's territory.

blow off *(verb)*
To cancel or fail to appear for. "Did you go to court for
that traffic ticket?" "No, I blew it off. I'll just pay the fine."

boatlift *(noun, also used as a verb)*
A means of transporting people, usually refugees, away
from danger. In 1982, thousands of Cubans were *boatlifted*
from their homeland to Florida in an exodus that came to
be known as the Mariel (for their port of embarkation)
boatlift. Individuals thus evacuated are known as "boat
people."

bonding *(noun)*
A cosmetic dental technique that disguises chipped or
stained teeth by adding an enamellike surface to the teeth.

box *(verb)*
Medical for *die*. "Any action in 612?" "Yeah. He boxed
around midnight."

breakdancing *(noun)*
An acrobatic form of dancing that includes such floor moves as spinning on the head, back, or hands; "poppin'," which involves sudden shoulder and arm movements; locking, or larger dance movements; *electric boogie* and the *moonwalk*. Extremely popular in inner-city and other U.S. areas in the mid-1980s.

B-strep *(noun)*
Abbreviation for Group B (beta hemolytic) streptococcus, a bacteria responsible for a growing percentage of deaths among newborn infants. The organism lives in the gastrointestinal tract and is sometimes passed on to the baby via the birth canal. Both men and women may be carriers of B-strep; current medical research indicates that the organism is probably sexually transmitted. If not treated in time, the infection is fatal for at least half of its victims.

bubble concept *(noun)*
An Environmental Protection Agency measurement that considers the total industrial pollution created by a factory rather than each individual contaminant. The concept envisions a bubble above the building that has a single aperture that vents all the effluvia released by the factory.

build-down *(noun)*
A plan to eliminate or slow down the arms race by ordering the destruction of one current weapon for each new one introduced.

bulletin-board system *(noun)*
A computer network accessible to anyone who has a computer and a modem (the device that makes it possible for a computer to use telephone lines). There are an estimated two thousand BBS's across the United States, carrying

input—editorials, movie reviews, travel tips, telephone numbers, etc.—from tens of thousands of computer fans. A BBS is operated by a *sysop*, or system operator.

bump and run *(noun)*
An option in football wherein a pass receiver may block a defensive player before going downfield to receive a pass.

busters *(noun)*
Ghostbusters, an extremely successful 1984 movie comedy about a team of spirit banishers, spawned echoes across the land: The presidential campaign produced "Reagan Busters" and "Fritz Busters"; New York City's traffic department mustered "Gridlock Busters"; federal and state drug administrations became "Drug Busters"; police departments, "Crime Busters"; department-store sales, "Inflation Busters" and a trademarked insecticide, "Roach Busters," to name a few.

CAD/CAM KAD-kam *(noun)*
Acronym for computer-aided design/computer-aided manufacturing, the computer systems that automate the drafting of mechanical and structural designs.

CAE *(noun)*
Abbreviation for computer-aided engineering, the combining of high-powered software with computerized work stations for the design of microprocessor chips and electronic systems.

cafeteria plan *(noun)*
A flexible benefit package offered by some corporations to their employees that makes alternative options available in addition to such basic benefits as health insurance. Within a specified dollar amount, workers are able to tailor their own benefits to include features ranging from cash to legal services to extra vacation time.

Cajun popcorn *(noun)*
Fried cornmeal batter containing flakes of shrimp, crab,

or crayfish. Cajun popcorn is a mainstay of Cajun cuisine, an increasingly popular, highly spiced type of food that was originated in the Louisiana bayous by descendants of the Arcadians—French Canadians who were driven out of Nova Scotia by the British in the eighteenth century.

camcorder *(noun)*
A battery-powered, hand-held videocamera/sound recorder. The combination device, unlike earlier camera/recorders, which came in two separate units, is a lightweight single unit that allows a user to record an event and play it back immediately.

camel *(verb)*
To act in an uninspired and bureaucratic manner. Based on the humorous definition of a camel: a horse designed by a committee. Columnist William Safire quotes a disparaging remark about unimaginative people who, "afraid of change," are likely to "camel an idea to death."

CAMP *(noun)*
Acronym for Campaign Against Marijuana Planting, an American state-local-federal task force whose field teams search out and destroy illegally raised cannabis crops.

caramel *(noun)*
Fuel for nuclear reactors, composed of low-grade, enriched uranium and so called because of its resemblance to caramel candy.

cash cow *(noun)*
An investment or business enterprise made for the purpose of providing revenue, as opposed to one made in order to create long-term growth.

cattle show *(noun)*
A public assembly of presidential candidates in a primary campaign; comparable to a beauty contest.

Cavaillon KAV-uh-yon *(noun)*
An intensely fragrant melon resembling a cantaloupe. First imported from France in 1984, Cavaillons became popular with elegant restaurants and their patrons despite their high price.

cellular phone *(noun)*
Mobile telephone, used with increasing frequency in cars. Cellular radio telephone systems have three components: the cell site, containing fixed radio equipment; the mobile telephone switching office (MTSO); and the mobile phone itself. Recent technological advances have permitted vastly enlarged use of cellular phones: "Within a decade," observed *The New York Times* in late 1984, "mobile phones could be as common as video cassettes today."

CEO *(noun)*
Trademark for a popular board game in which players advance up the pyramid of success (to become CEO: chief executive officer) by fall of the dice and the ability to answer business trivia questions.

chatcom *(noun)*
A radio or TV talk show whose main thrust is comedy; Johnny Carson's *Tonight* show is an example.

checkbook journalism *(noun)*
The reporting of news obtained through the payment of a fee for information; the phrase is usually one of contempt, implying the use of a less-than-straightforward means of gathering news.

checkbook witness *(noun)*
An expert who is paid by defense or prosecution to provide information at a court trial.

chicken hawk *(noun)*
A homosexual male, middle-aged or older, who is attracted to and seeks out boys and very young men.

chilling effect *(noun)*
Most often used for the inhibiting of the press by court decisions imposing heavy damages against publications found guilty of libel-law violations.

chip revolution *(noun)*
The technological advance that replaced vacuum tubes and transistor electronic circuitry with integrated circuits and chips in microelectronic systems.

chlamydia kluh-MID-ee-uh *(noun)*
A venereal disease more common in the United States than any other sexually transmitted disease. Chlamydia strikes up to 10 million Americans a year. "Like herpes," noted *Time* in early 1985, chlamydia "is rapidly becoming the bane of the middle class; up to 10 percent of all college students are afflicted with it. Says Dr. Mary Guinan of the Centers for Disease Control, 'Chlamydia is the disease of the '80s.'" One method of detecting the ailment is a trademarked diagnostic test called *MicroTrak*.

chop shop *(noun)*
An automotive garage where stolen cars are stripped and disassembled to be sold as parts.

circuit breaker *(noun)*
An economic device designed to provide relief from high tax rates for low-income property owners by income tax rebates. (From the electric circuit breaker that protects against current overload.)

clonidine *(noun)*
An experimental drug reported to have marked success in curbing smokers' cigarette cravings. "Researchers," reported *Business Week*, "say the drug stops the urge [to smoke] directly by acting on those cells in the brain that are associated with addiction."

communications satellite *(noun)*
An orbiting space device that retransmits signals received from earth to other receiving points over a broad area.

community channels *(noun)*
Cable TV channels accessible to interested citizens and civic groups for locally originated programming and inexpensive local advertising.

compact disk *(noun)*
A grooveless digital sound recording from which the signal is picked up by a laser beam and fed to an amplifier, free of interference and distortion. Also called a *CD*.

computer commuter *(noun)*
(See *electronic cottage*.)

computer hedgehog *(noun)*
An individual whose computer knowledge is limited to only one type of machine, activity, or set of programs.

computerist *(noun)*
An individual proficient in the operation of a computer.

computer monitoring *(noun)*
A management process for checking employee performance by connecting factory or office work stations to computers that count and record such activities as keystrokes per hour or time spent using telephone lines. In 1985, *U.S. News and World Report* predicted that by 1990 more than half of the 40 million U.S. workers expected to be using video display terminals (VDTs) by that date will be subject to computer monitoring. While many employers are enthusiastic about the advantages of the practice, many employees are not. One union steward, for example, reflecting a widely held worker opinion, said, "It's like Big Brother is watching you."

Contadora kon-tuh-DOR-uh *(adjective)*
A group or a philosophical approach favoring peaceful negotiation to settle Central American political disputes, especially those between Nicaragua and El Salvador. (The creators of the approach, the foreign ministers of Colombia, Venezuela, Panama, and Mexico, met on Contadora Island, off the coast of Panama, in 1983.)

contra *(noun)*
A member of a guerrilla group bent on destroying Nicaragua's *Sandinista* government. *Contra* is a contraction of the Spanish word *contrario*: opponent or enemy.

cooler *(noun)*
A drink, usually marketed in bottles, that contains a mixture of wine and fruit juice.

cosmoceutical *(noun)*
A prescription cosmetic dispensed or ordered by a dermatologist to improve both the appearance and the health of the skin.

Cosmograd *(noun)*
A 110-ton Soviet space station with a projected 1985 launching date. The station, scheduled to be placed in orbit by a 300-foot rocket, will reportedly accommodate up to a dozen scientific and military researchers.

coyote *(noun)*
A person who engages in the smuggling of illegal immigrants from Latin America into the United States. The aliens, with no recourse to the authorities for fear of exposure, often become victims of exploitation by the coyotes.

cracker *(noun)*
(See *hacker*.)

critical path *(noun)*
A management technique, its name taken from science, that employs computers to determine the fastest and most efficient way to chart and control complex projects.

cross-dressing *(noun)*
An androgynous fashion style involving the wearing, by both sexes, of clothes, hairstyles, and makeup formerly considered the exclusive province of either men or women. *The New York Times* noted in a late 1984 report from London that "the men in Mohawk hairdos are wearing eye makeup as elaborate as Elizabeth Taylor's in *Cleopatra*."

cross-training *(noun)*
An exercise system in which several sports—e.g., tennis, running, and swimming—are regularly practiced in order to produce balanced muscular development and generalized physical fitness.

cruciverbalist *(noun)*
A devotee of or expert at crossword puzzles.

cryobirth *(noun)*
The birth of an organism from a frozen embryo.

cryptozoology *(noun)*
The attempt to find and study mysterious creatures such as the Loch Ness Monster and the abominable snowman.

dancercise *(noun)*
Conditioning exercise in the form of rhythmic dancing, usually in groups.

DBS *(noun)*
Abbreviation for direct broadcast satellite, a system in which television signals are sent directly to *satellite antennas* from a satellite.

debit card *(noun)*
A small plastic card that closely resembles a credit card in appearance but that functions like a checkbook. The cost of an item purchased with a debit card is usually deducted electronically from the purchaser's checking account almost immediately.

deep pocket *(noun)*
Legal slang for the party in a lawsuit with the most money. "The spouse with the assets—the 'deep pocket,' as he's

known in the matrimonial trade—tries to divulge as little information as possible" (*New York* magazine).

defcon *(noun)*
Acronym for defense condition, a state of military alert. There are five stages, ranging from defcon I (war) to defcon V (a peacetime stage of combat readiness when military forces have no expectation of imminent attack).

dense pack *(noun)*
A proposed system of MX silo construction in tight clusters, which, the system's supporters contend, would cause incoming enemy missiles to destroy one another before impacting.

devastator bullet *(noun)*
An exploding small-caliber bullet brought to national attention when used by John Hinckley in his assassination attempt on President Ronald Reagan in 1981.

dirty rice *(noun)*
An important item in Cajun cuisine, composed of boiled rice mixed with herbs, spices, and finely chopped chicken livers. (See also *Cajun popcorn.*)

dorky *(adjective)*
Slow, not very bright. *Christine*, said *Time*, was a "tense tale of a dorky teenager whose 20-year-old Plymouth has an evil will of its own."

downscale *(adjective)*
Inferior, in a social or income-level sense.

Dungeons and Dragons *(noun)*
A trademarked role-playing strategy game in which players

with "magical powers" seek fortunes in a perilous maze guarded by mythical and occult monsters.

dustman *(noun)*
An advocate of the theory that the planets of the solar system were created by the accretion of galactic dust in the sun's gravitational field.

EAS *(noun)*
Abbreviation for electronic article surveillance, used by retail stores to prevent would-be shoplifters from carrying merchandise out of the store. An EAS system attaches a tag, which is removed at the time of purchase, to each piece of merchandise; if not detached, the tag will electronically trigger an alarm radio at the exit.

ECU EK-yoo *(noun)*
Acronym for European Currency Unit. There is no actual ECU coin or bill; the unit, which is made up of nine separate national currencies, is used principally in currency markets by countries aiming to stabilize their own currencies. It is also used as a means of payment among members of the European Economic Community.

electric boogie *(noun)*
A form of breakdancing in which the performer appears to have an electric current passing through his body, and in which arm and body waves and *moonwalks* are included.

electrofunk *(noun)*
Funk music played on electronically amplified instruments.

electronic cottage *(noun)*
A worker's home when it is used as a computer-linked workplace. A home worker in an electronic cottage (a spin-off from "cottage industry") is known as a *telecommuter* or *computer commuter*.

electronic mail *(noun)*
Letters composed on word processors or personal computers that are electronically transmitted to a receiving terminal via telephone lines. Electronic letters are being used with increasing frequency by corporations, which employ electronic mail services to transmit their correspondence.

English creep *(noun)*
The spread of English as an international language. *U.S. News & World Report* observed that in 1985 "English has become to the modern world what Latin was to the ancients, dominating the planet as *the* medium of exchange in science, technology, commerce, tourism, diplomacy, and pop culture. So wide is its sweep that 345 million people use English as their first language and an additional 400 million as their second."

EOE *(noun)*
Abbreviation for equal opportunity employer, one that has pledged not to discriminate on the basis of sex, race, age, etc., when hiring or promoting personnel.

ergometer *(noun)*
A rowing machine with adjustable resistance that closely simulates water resistance; used for training rowing teams in the winter and for general exercise by fitness fans.

ETS *(noun)*
Abbreviation for environmental tobacco smoke. "Periodically," said the R. J. Reynolds Tobacco Company in a 1985 advertisement, "the public hears about an individual scientific study which claims to show that ETS may be harmful to non-smokers." (See also *passive smoking*.)

Euromissile *(noun)*
An intermediate-range missile deployed in Europe on both sides of the Iron Curtain.

evil empire *(noun)*
A phrase used by President Ronald Reagan in a 1983 speech to refer to the Soviet Union. The "evil empire approach" has come to mean an automatically hostile stance toward the U.S.S.R., which is held responsible for most of the world's problems.

exit poll *(noun)*
A survey of voters as they leave the polling place so that the news organizations can establish the trend of an election before the polls close.

facedness *(noun)*
The tendency of one side or the other of the human face to be dominant. The study of facedness is relatively recent; early reports indicate, however, that in left-faced people, for example, the left eye is lower than the right and the lines and dimples of the left side are the most distinct. One scientist who studies facedness, Dr. Karl Smith of the University of Wisconsin, says his research confirms that "all persons have a sort of facial fingerprint . . . just as they have distinctive patterns of right or left handedness."

factory farming *(noun)*
The practice of raising such food animals as sheep, hogs, and chickens in sterile and automated operations that more closely resemble factories than traditional farms.

Fannie Mae *(noun)*
Acronym for the Federal National Mortgage Association, which, like *Ginnie Mae* and *Freddie Mac*, aims to increase funds available for mortgages.

fast burn *(noun)*
A system designed to reduce fuel consumption in gasoline engines through more rapid ignition, which increases the heat and compression in the cylinder with a smaller amount of gasoline.

fifth-generation computer *(noun)*
A highly advanced robotic computer programmed with the ability to "think" and to arrive at solutions to complex problems much as a human being would.

first-sale doctrine *(noun)*
A federal law permitting the purchaser of a product to resell or rent the product. First-sale doctrine was a widely heard phrase in the 1984 controversy about the leasing of film cassettes by retailers; film studios went to court in an effort to halt such rentals, from which they received no royalties.

first strike *(noun)*
The opening move in a war, particularly in a nuclear conflict. Prevailing military opinion holds that the winner of such a war would be the nation that made the first strike, or attack, on its enemy's land-based missiles and nuclear-armed aircraft, thus crippling the enemy's retaliatory capabilities.

Flashing *(noun)*
A trademarked electronic device developed in France that is said to eliminate the guesswork in selecting sexual partners. The pocket-size gadget, which is available in four wavelengths (identifying its owner as heterosexual, homosexual male or female, or interested in swapping partners), beeps when it comes within ten feet of someone carrying a *Flashing* tuned to the same frequency. If the one so contacted is not pleasing to the beholder, says the man-

ufacturer, the machine can be switched off until its owner is out of range. "Le Flashing," first marketed in Paris in 1984, was introduced in the United States via Los Angeles in early 1985.

flutter *(verb)*
To administer a lie-detector, or polygraph, test; from the test's measurements of a subject's nervousness, which may reveal guilt. Commenting on a large-scale test of the polygraph by the Defense Department in 1985, columnist William Safire refers to the device as "a modern instrument of mental torture" and asserts that "to force it on a suspect is to give him the Fourth Degree." The department, he continues, "can now flutter thousands of scared employees," which could "lead to the demand that tens of thousands of citizens submit to fluttering as a test of their patriotism."

focus group *(noun)*
A panel of "typical people" questioned by market researchers or pollsters in order to learn the reactions and feelings of those questioned about subjects of interest to the questioners. Focus group interviewees are frequently observed by researchers through two-way mirrors.

football *(noun)*
Military jargon for the briefcase carried constantly by a member of one of the four branches of the U.S. armed services who is always close to the president. The *football*—which, obviously, must not be dropped—contains the codes needed to launch all U.S. missiles.

footprint *(noun)*
The area in which a particular TV broadcasting satellite's signal can be received.

Fortune 500 *(noun)*
A list of the leading U.S. industrial companies, printed annually in the business magazine *Fortune*. It has come to signify big business in general, Walter Mondale's meaning when he said during his run for the presidency in 1984, "I would rather fight for the heart and soul of America than fight for the bonuses of the Fortune 500."

401 (k) Plan *(noun)*
A retirement plan offered to employees by some employers. Similar to IRA and Keogh plans, the 401 (k) allows employees to contribute pretax dollars whose taxes are deferred until the funds are withdrawn. These taxes may then be spread over ten years. The plan permits depositers to withdraw money early without penalties under hardship circumstances.

fourth degree *(noun)*
(See *flutter*.)

Freddie Mac *(noun)*
The name commonly used for the Federal Home Mortgage Corporation, which buys, on behalf of the government, conventional residential mortgages from lenders and sells mortgage securities to other major investors. Freddie Mac, which by 1984 had bought $91.5 billion in mortgages and sold $82 billion in mortgage securities, has been called a major force in attracting new money to housing.

freezenik FREEZ-nik *(noun)*
A supporter of a moratorium, or "freeze," on the manufacture and use of nuclear weapons.

fuzzword *(noun)*
An apparently precise word that nevertheless confuses

communication; elegant gobbledegook that gives the impression of clarity and sense while deliberately obfuscating. Sometimes fuzzwords, because of their frequent appearance in the nation's capital, are called "the language of the Potomac," an example of which is the government's use of "revenue enhancement" when it means "tax increase."

gamer *(noun)*
A player in football—and, occasionally, in other sports—known for playing the entire game full-out regardless of injuries or setbacks; one who plays despite pain.

Gang of Four *(noun)*
Four Chinese officials who were held responsible for the elimination or demotion of thousands of intellectuals and professionals alleged to have introduced Western influences into Chinese culture, and to have sabotaged Mao Tse-tung's *Great Leap Forward*. "Gang of..." has become widely used as a label for a group of any size accused of anything.

gateway drug *(noun)*
A recreational mood-changing substance (e.g., marijuana) that is not medically classified as habit-forming or potentially deadly but that may lead its users into experimentation with more potent substances, such as heroin.

gender gap *(noun)*
The difference between the perceptions (usually of a politician or political issue) of men and women. The phrase was widely used during the 1984 presidential election campaign, in which the Republicans were initially concerned about the apparently negative view of Ronald Reagan held by women.

gene therapy *(noun)*
The experimental technique of replacing a defective gene (the element that controls hereditary character) with a laboratory-created gene; used in treating single-gene diseases, such as cystic fibrosis.

geostationary satellite *(noun)*
A communications satellite that, placed in orbit above the equator, stays above the same point on the earth's surface.

getaway special *(noun)*
A small cargo payload carried aboard space shuttles. Two sizes of cylindrical container are available for rent by NASA (five and two-and-a-half cubic feet) for the transport into space of a great variety of experiments in the effects of weightlessness.

ghetto blaster *(noun)*
A large, portable, stereophonic radio/tape player, popular with inner-city youth.

Ginnie Mae *(noun)*
Acronym for the Government National Mortgage Association, which was created by Congress to increase money available for mortgages by pooling bank-generated mortgages, guaranteeing them, and turning them into secu-

rities that pass the home buyer's principal and interest payments on to the investor.

gîte zheet *(noun)*
A private country vacation home in France. One- to two-week rentals of gîtes are increasingly popular with vacationing Americans, who occupy residences in areas such as Normandy, Brittany, the Loire Valley, and the French Mediterranean coast at rates ranging from $103 to $375 a week.

global village *(noun)*
The theoretical concept of the world reduced in size by modern communications and transportation to a single community of neighbors with interlocking interests and needs.

golden handcuffs *(noun)*
A contract between a company and an incoming executive that guarantees the executive rewards he would lose on departure, thereby creating a financial incentive for loyalty. Sometimes called "diamond handcuffs."

golden handshake *(noun)*
A lucrative severance agreement given to a fired employee, usually a high-salaried executive.

golpe GOLE-pay *(noun)*
The sudden overthrow of a government; a coup d'etat; the Spanish word for "blow" or "strike," golpe is generally used in connection with Latin American countries.

gomer GO-mur *(noun)*
Acronym for "get out of my emergency room." Medical slang for a patient with inappropriate requests or medically

unsolvable problems who persistently applies for emergency hospital treatment.

goonda GOON-duh *(noun)*
A young thug, or hoodlum. *Goonda* is used principally about or in India, which is also the source of *thug*, a member of a gang of professional robbers who strangled their victims. The English word *goon*, whose meaning is close to the Indian *goonda*, comes, however, from a different source: it is a shortened form of *gooney*, which once meant "fool."

Gore-Tex *(noun)*
Trademarked name for a waterproof, windproof fabric widely used in the manufacture of outdoor garments and camping equipment. Laminated with microporous Teflon, which will pass water vapor from perspiration outward but not pass water droplets inward, the fabric is thus both "breathable" and waterproof.

gorilla *(noun)*
A block-busting or extremely high-powered and best-selling film or record, in entertainment industry argot.

granola *(noun)*
Updated word for "bohemian": an individual whose lifestyle is earthy, unconventional, and self-designed. A granola, named for the rough-textured nut-and-grain food he or she often favors, is also—for the same reason—called a "crunchy chewy."

gravlaks GRAHV-lox *(noun)*
Swedish-style salmon marinated in dill, salt, and pepper, and served thinly sliced with mustard sauce.

gray market (noun)
The trade in foreign goods purchased by U.S. retailers directly from the manufacturer's representative overseas, rather than from the manufacturer's more expensive American subsidiary or distributor. When the U.S. dollar is strong, gray market merchandise, which can include stereo equipment, cameras, watches, and tires, is often sold at 20 percent to 40 percent less than its usual price; the problem for consumers is that such merchandise is almost never covered by a manufacturer's warranty or guarantee.

grazing (noun)
The practice of enjoying, according to Johns Hopkins anthropologist Sidney W. Mintz, "brief, meallike interventions throughout the day," or, as another authority put it, "eating hummingbird-style, a little bit here, a little bit there." *The New York Times* observed that grazing, "which seems to be spreading throughout the United States, has excited the food-service industry and caused Chinese take-out restaurants and street-side vendors alike to flourish." "Heavy grazers," adds *Advertising Age*, "are the most active consumers going." The publication reports that these people buy more appliances, cars, clothing, new houses, and other consumer products and are more likely to be optimistic about the nation's economy than their "non-grazing counterparts."

Great Leap Forward (noun)
Chinese leader Mao Tse-tung's accelerated industrialization and rural collectivization program, in place from 1958 to 1961; often called simply the "great leap." The program's name is currently used to label any radical, fast-moving plan for cultural or economic change.

greenmail *(noun)*
The inflated price paid by a company, in an effort to avoid takeover by a corporate raider, for the raider's stock in the company. "[The raider] bought a major stake in the company, trying for a quick greenmail profit" (*The New York Times*). Greenmail is an offshoot of *blackmail*, defined in *The Random House College Dictionary* as "payment extorted by intimidation."

Greens *(noun)*
The increasingly influential West German political party whose basic platform rests on environmentalism and whose aim is to detach West Germany from NATO in order to set the nation on a path of neutralism. The Greens, whose principal constituency is among the young, are supported, according to historian Hans-Peter Schwarz, by voters who are "antiauthoritarian, critical toward representative democracy, hedonistic and frequently opposed to the traditional concept of family, ... critical of modern technology and ... upset and dissatisfied with the state, if not openly opposed to it."

greenshoe *(noun)*
The right of the general partner in a limited partnership to raise additional money without the legal requirement to issue a new prospectus. "The offering was capitalized at $50 million, with a *greenshoe* to $65 million" (from a letter from Ferris & Co. broker E. L. Johnson).

greyhound *(noun)*
A very fast basketball player.

grumpie *(noun)*
A label coined by car makers and their advertising agencies

for a member of that market segment that buys 43 percent of all new automobiles: "The grown-up, mature person," a well-to-do individual over the age of fifty.

Guardian Angels *(noun)*

A controversial group of young, unarmed volunteers who patrol the New York City subways and high-crime areas in some other cities to deter crime and make, on occasion, citizen's arrests. Popular with many subway riders, who say they feel safer with the "Angels" around, the group's members are considered by some law-enforcement professionals to be dangerous amateurs and vigilantes.

hacker *(noun)*
A dedicated *computerist*. Frequently, a computer expert who illegally enters guarded data bases, often via telephone connections. "The hackers' code," observed *The New York Times*, is "a strange blend of radicalism and technology," holding that "all the wonders that electronic technology can perform should belong to all the people, as should the right to explore this technology unfettered." One dedicated hacker described his ilk as someone who "hacks away at a computer until a program does what he wants it to do." A specific type of hacker is the *cracker*; one who uses his skills to break into computer security systems simply for his own amusement.

hair extension *(noun)*
The attachment of real or synthetic hairpieces to the head by a process that combines braiding, gluing, and burning.

hat trick *(noun)*
The achievement of three desirable goals in succession;

from the sports term meaning three wins or goals in one game by a single player.

head hunter *(noun)*
1. In football, a defense player (usually a defensive back or linebacker) who looks for opportunities to intimidate runners or pass receivers by landing hard shots to their heads (also known as "ringing a player's bell"). 2. In baseball, a pitcher who often tries to intimidate batters by throwing the ball at their heads.

Helsinki Agreement *(noun)*
The human rights doctrine signed by the countries of Europe in 1975 after a two-year conference in Helsinki, Finland. Rights listed in the agreement include freedom from government religious persecution. *Helsinki Watch* is an organization that monitors observance of the agreement.

high-five *(noun)*
An exuberant overhead slapping of right hands between two individuals that expresses congratulatory high spirits and camaraderie. High-fives began in the world of sports ("Tigers outfielder Kirk Gibson exchanged high-five salutes with jubilant teammates after hitting a two-run homer...."—Collier's *Year Book*) but is now a commonly seen gesture: "...a bad African prince who likes to give American high-fives" (*Newsweek*).

hip-hop *(noun)*
A popular musical idiom also known as "rap," a form of street music that originated in New York City along with *breakdancing*. Hip-hop, which *New York Times* music critic Robert Palmer called "an international phenomenon" in early 1985, consists of two or more performers trading

rhymes or catch phrases, accompanied by music and/or electronic effects.

human resources *(noun)*
Personnel management.

Hummer *(noun)*
Trademarked name of a new, high-mobility, multipurpose wheeled vehicle now in production for the U.S. armed forces. A one-and-a-quarter-ton payload machine of exceptional mobility and versatility, the Hummer is reported to handle off-road terrain with ease, climbing sixty-degree grades, fording rivers five feet deep, and conquering knee-high boulders. With different body configurations on one basic body chassis, it fulfills many specialized functions— cargo/troop carrier, ambulance, or weapons carrier.

hypermarket *(noun)*
A huge store combining a supermarket and a department store. Cincinnati's new Bigg's is an example of the species, which appears to be ready to proliferate in the United States. "This bustling store," commented *The New York Times* of Bigg's, "which is one and a half times the length of a football field, sells everything from cucumbers to computers, poultry to pocketbooks, eclairs to exercise bicycles. . . . Bigg's is as much of a jump from the typical supermarket as the supermarket was from the mom and pop grocery."

infomercial *(noun)*
A cable television program, commonly running for fifteen minutes, that combines short commercials with information relevant to the product or service being advertised and that resembles a conventional cable TV show. An infomercial is a first cousin to an *advertorial*.

insider trading *(noun)*
The purchase or sale of a company's stock by an individual possessing nonpublic, special knowledge of the company's affairs. The Insider Trading Sanctions Act of 1984 makes such transactions a federal offense.

intelligent *(adjective)*
Having computerized abilities to effect changes; increasingly used to describe a machine, building, or device that has the built-in capacity to make necessary adjustments, e.g., the camera that judges its own light and distance requirements and sets itself accordingly.

interactive cable *(noun)*
A system that can carry signals both to and from cable TV subscribers. Also called two-way cable or "upstream communication" (because the flow of information is also from the home to the broadcaster), this system has been used experimentally for such purposes as conducting viewer polls.

IRMA UR-muh *(noun)*
Acronym for individual retirement mortgage account. (See *reverse mortgage*.)

item veto *(noun)*
The rejection of a single section in a bill otherwise made into law by the signature of a chief executive. Such selective removal of individual items in legislation is also called a line veto.

Jarvik 7 *(noun)*
The first artificial heart ever implanted in a human patient. Invented by Dr. Robert Jarvik and constructed of plastic, the heart was not self-contained but depended on an outside, portable power source.

Jazzercise *(noun)*
Trademark for a popular form of exercise movements performed to the beat of jazz music.

job shop *(noun)*
A company that leases professional, experienced, and highly skilled help to businesses, often on a per-project basis. Because many corporations have undergone roller-coaster cycles of prosperity and slump in recent years, many are finding it less expensive to lease employees than to hire them permanently. "Leasing from job shops allows us to work at full capacity without having a long-term responsibility to these employees," observed one corporate man-

ager. Employees leased from job shops are called *job shoppers*.

junk bond *(noun)*
In financial jargon, an often unsecured, low-grade, high-yield debt security, rated BB or lower by credit agencies. Junk bonds are commonly issued by indebted companies to raise money to repay debts or to reorganize. Their high-yield results from their high risk.

just-in-time *(noun)*
An innovative production management and quality-control technique developed in Japan (where it is called *kanban*) that is coming into increasingly wide use in the United States. *Just-in-time* is based on minimum inventory, careful planning, and total quality control. It calls for the elimination of stockpiles of production parts and finished goods. All materials are in active use as part of work in progress, arriving just in time to be assembled into finished products, just in time to be sold. "Just-in-time makes manufacturing a competitive weapon," said *Forbes* magazine.

kanban KAN-ban *(noun)*
(See *just-in-time*.)

Kevlar *(noun)*
A gold-colored aramid fiber developed and trademarked by the DuPont Corporation for use as tire cord. Kevlar is finding increased application in boat building, where it is used in the manner of fiberglass, to which it is said to be superior in lightness and strength. Kevlar is also used in the manufacture of bulletproof vests.

key *(adjective)*
Very good, the best. "He plays key trumpet."

Klezmer music *(noun)*
A form of Yiddish folk music, originally played by traveling musicians (Klezmorim) and wedding jesters in Central Europe and currently enjoying a wave of revived popularity in the United States.

LA *(adjective)*
Abbreviation for light/low alcohol; usually applied to beer or wine.

Laffer curve *(noun)*
A mathematical formula demonstrating the effects of tax rates on economic activity. Devised by economist Arthur Laffer, the curve purports to show that the productivity generated by massive tax reductions would result in strong overall economic growth, subsequently bringing in higher tax revenues at lower rates.

la langue du Coca-Cola luh LAHNG doo ko-kuh-KO-luh *(noun)*
A scoffing French term for the English language.

LBO *(noun)*
Abbreviation for leveraged buyout, a transaction in which a small group of investors buys a company with largely borrowed funds. The debt is eventually repaid with income

produced by the acquired company's operations or by the sale of its assets.

legs *(noun)*
Staying power, usually applied to films. "*Scarface* broke out with a roar over the weekend, but some distributors are skeptical about the movie's legs" (New York *Post*).

lemon law *(noun)*
Legislation, usually enacted by a state legislature, that is designed to protect consumers who have purchased defective new cars. Most states' lemon laws guarantee the purchaser free repairs on his vehicle within its warranty period, if the repairs are needed to correct defects present at the time of sale.

Liberation theology *(noun)*
A radical interpretation of Christian teachings that has prompted increased social activism among Catholic priests and nuns in Latin America. Proponents of the doctrine, which employs Marxist analysis, assert that it is a function of the church to assist in bringing about economic and political change in the Third World.

light infantry *(noun)*
Modern U.S. Army units of soldiers that are not attached to tank or armored personnel carrier units and that are equipped with fewer helicopters and artillery pieces than mechanized infantry divisions. The army, which created four new light divisions in 1984 as part of its major modernization program, said its main reason for doing so was to have a large force with the ability to move overseas more rapidly than conventional heavy divisions. (In the eighteenth and nineteenth centuries, light infantry troops

were those who carried rifles and who could thus march more quickly than their heavy-musket armed colleagues.)

linear thinking *(noun)*
A type of formal logic that, according to *New York Times* columnist William Safire, is "a brand of thinking that moves steadily from cause to effect to the next cause and so on."

line extension *(noun)*
A marketing term for a new product designed to capitalize on the acceptance of an old, familiar product. Ivory Shampoo, for example, is a line extension of Ivory Soap. Such spinoff products are also known to merchandisers as *flankers*.

liquidity trap *(noun)*
A condition of the economy that results from the unavailability of long-term loans. In a liquidity trap, a company is unlikely to be able to raise enough money for long-term expansion or construction.

lockbox *(noun)*
A device that enables cable television subscribers to block out channels they do not wish their children to watch.

log off *(verb)*
To sign off or terminate one's access to a computer bank or data base. Opposite of *log on*, to enter a computer network legally, as opposed to *hacking*.

loopy *(adjective)*
Eccentric, daffy, slightly crazy. "*Fitzcarraldo*," wrote screenwriter/critic Kevin Scott of Werner Herzog's complex and difficult-to-produce movie, "is Mr. Herzog's loopy tribute to his own doggedness in making the film."

mail merging *(noun)*
The automatic production of "personalized" form letters by a word processor using disk-stored information in conjunction with a mailing list.

male bonding *(noun)*
The formation of close personal relationships and loyalties among men.

Marfan syndrome *(noun)*
An inherited disorder of connective tissue, also called the Lincoln syndrome. Marfan, which affects twenty thousand Americans, is characterized by the loose-jointedness and elongated limbs that distinguished the appearance of Abraham Lincoln, who, many doctors now believe, was a Marfan sufferer. Because the syndrome also severely damages its victims' aortic valves, it once killed most of them; new techniques that include the use of beta blockers and aortic valve replacement have improved and lengthened many Marfan patients' lives.

marital rape *(noun)*
Forcible sexual intercourse within a marriage; recognized as a criminal act by courts of law during the mid-1980s.

maximinimalism *(noun)*
An art movement that teaches that every little thing, when placed on a big thing, is art. In its 1984 catalogue, the New York University art department observes that the max-iminimalist school began when French artist Sylvain Tati "made a small dot in the center of a [huge] canvas with a marker pen while crying, 'C'est l'art!'"

mechatronics *(noun)*
From *mecha*nics and elec*tronics*. The branch of engineering that seeks to synthesize computer and mechanical engineering in the automation of industry.

mediagenic *(adjective)*
Having a personality and appearance that attract wide coverage by television and the print media.

medigap *(noun)*
The part of medical costs not covered by the federal Medicare program, which provides health insurance to people over the age of sixty-five and to certain disabled individuals. Medigap insurance is a private supplementary policy covering health-care expenses that are not reimbursed by Medicare.

me generation *(noun)*
A label much used for the *baby boomers* during the 1970s, a decade characterized by charismatic religions, self-help movements, and an obsessive search for individual fulfillment and happiness. Its slogan might have been "watch out for number one."

mego *(noun)*
Acronym for "mine eyes glaze over." Used humorously, a *mego* is an event, performance, or piece of writing or art that produces dazed boredom in the observer. Also used adjectivally, as in "the mego factor."

menu *(noun)*
A list of the programs available in a computer service. *Menu-driven* means that all programs will be presented for selection in logical order, in contrast to command-driven, which means the user must supply his own directions to the computer.

micromanagement *(noun)*
The detailed planning of localized operations by a central executive; most commonly used to refer to the military, when top commanders and civilian officials, usually apart from and prior to a military operation, set out minutely particularized orders that allow little or no decision-making by the officers on the scene of the battle. *The Wall Street Journal* noted that the 1983 U.S. invasion of Grenada marked "a significant move away from the micromanagement that some analysts think has plagued American operations, particularly the Iranian hostage rescue mission."

MicroTrak *(noun)*
(See *chlamydia*.)

midlife crisis *(noun)*
The period of anxiety often experienced by people between the ages of forty and fifty, which author Gail Sheehy (*Passages*) called "that apostrophe in time between the end of growing up and the beginning of growing old."

mini-RPV *(noun)*
An RPV is a remotely piloted vehicle. A mini-RPV is a small, remote-controlled drone aircraft that carries a television camera and is used in combat reconnaissance.

minivan *(noun)*
A trimmed-down version of the conventional, boxlike van. An automotive bestseller in the mid-1980s, the minivan's sudden popularity, especially among *yuppies*, was attributed to such features as its relatively low operating costs, good mileage, copious interior space, and trendy, "aerodynamic" appearance. Minivan manufacturers expected to sell 600,000 to 700,000 units by 1986 in the United States, a nation that, commented the *Wall Street Journal*, "has gone minicrazy."

minoxidil muh-NOX-uh-dil *(noun)*
A prescription drug whose success in restoring hair to balding heads was widely reported in 1984. Minoxidil, a clear liquid originally developed to treat high blood pressure, was approved by the FDA for that use, but its approval and marketing as a hair-growing agent is not expected by its manufacturer before 1987.

misery index *(noun)*
A figure used to denote a population's general level of economic distress, derived by adding the unemployment rate and the rate of inflation, as indicated by the consumer-price index.

MMDA *(noun)*
Abbreviation of money market deposit account.

monster man *(noun)*
A defensive back or linebacker who, having no set defensive assignment, roams the field in whichever direction the play dictates, gobbling up ball carriers and receivers.

moonwalk *(noun)*
A breakdancing step in which the performer, by shifting weight from one foot to the other and gliding backward, produces the illusion of walking forward; Michael Jackson, among others, is celebrated for his moonwalk.

motormouth *(noun)*
An informal pejorative appellation for an individual who talks frequently, rapidly, and at length.

mousse *(noun)*
1. A foam hairstyling preparation named for its resemblance to the whipped cream-based dessert. 2. The foamy mass created by the admixture of oil and water in an oil spill.

movideo *(noun)*
(See *rocumentary*.)

MTSO *(noun)*
Abbreviation for mobile telephone switching office. (See *cellular phone*.)

MTV *(noun)*
Abbreviation for Music Television, a cable network that shows *rock videos*.

muppie *(noun)*
Acronym for middle-aged urban professional; a spinoff from *yuppie* and *yumpie*. In early 1985 Mayor Barbara Sigmund of Princeton, New Jersey, decried what she called the "muppie invasion" of her town. "It's getting so you can't go to a luncheonette," she complained, "without having those damn plants hanging down in your face." Sigmund also noted that phenomena accompanying a muppie influx are what she called "terminal cutesification," "boutiqueification," and "bankification."

NDE *(noun)*
Abbreviation for near-death experience, an event reportedly undergone by some people who have recovered from apparent death. Individuals claiming to have had an NDE frequently describe God, heaven, or other phenomena associated with the afterlife.

neocon *(noun)*
Shortened form of neoconservative.

neoliberal *(noun)*
The label adopted by a loose confederation of former New Deal-style liberals who, while remaining loyal to the traditional liberal goals, are looking critically at the institutions associated with achieving them, such as organized labor and big government, and more sympathetically at such former foes as business and the military.

net-net *(adjective)*
Final; the last word; the conclusion reached after all elements have been added and subtracted. "The net-net software picture, then, is a bright one" (*New Haven Register*).

nomenklatura no-men-klah-TOO-ruh *(noun)*
The secret personnel and job-description list in the Soviet governing bureaucracy from which key people are selected for new positions and advancement.

nonbank NON-bank *(noun)*
A limited-service banking operation that eludes the federal prohibition of interstate banking by restricting its activities to the offering of either commercial loans or checking accounts but not both.

nopalitos no-puh-LEE-tohs *(noun)*
Leaves from the nopal cactus; newly popular in gourmet circles when battered and deep-fried as "tempura Mexicana" or as a salad ingredient.

nose candy *(noun)*
Slang for cocaine.

no-till *(noun)*
A farming technique that eliminates the plowing-under of the residue of the previous crop. No-till farmers simply plant under the residue in the spring, thereby reducing erosion and cutting fuel and equipment expenses.

nuclear waste *(noun)*
The spent but still highly radioactive fuel from nuclear power plants.

nuclear winter *(noun)*
The hypothetical season that would be permanently imposed on the earth following a nuclear war. A nuclear winter, in which sunlight would be severely limited by smoke and dust, would have bitterly cold temperatures, eventually extinguishing whatever life forms had survived the war's initial blasts.

omnicide *(noun)*
Literally, the killing of everything living, as in the hypothetical sterilization of the earth in a nuclear holocaust.

oncogene *(noun)*
A gene that apparently acts in originating cancer when its normal function in regulating growth is disrupted.

opportunistic infection *(noun)*
An illness developed in an individual suffering from acquired immune deficiency syndrome (AIDS), an immune-system disorder primarily afflicting male homosexuals, intravenous drug users, and hemophiliacs.

optical processor *(noun)*
A computer—still in the developmental stage—powered by light instead of silicon circuitry. Optical computers will, according to their developers, be faster, lighter, and cheaper than comparable silicon processors.

outsourcing *(noun)*
The practice by manufacturers of using product components or services that originate outside their own companies. *Outsource* is also used as a verb, as in "General Motors outsourced most of the parts for the new model."

Pac-man maneuver *(noun)*
A corporate ploy wherein one company, threatened with takeover by another, moves to acquire the would-be acquirer. Named for Pac-man, the round yellow creature in the trademarked computer game of the same name, whose object is to devour his adversaries before they can devour him.

passive smoking *(noun)*
The involuntary inhalation of tobacco smoke that occurs when a nonsmoker is exposed to the airborne nicotine produced by a nearby smoker. Exhaled smoke from another's cigarette, cigar, or pipe is sometimes called *ETS* (environmental tobacco smoke), *secondhand smoke*, or *sidestream smoke*. Among the substances a passive smoker inhales are radioactive particles called *radon daughters*.

pay-per-view *(noun)*
A type of pay cable TV in which subscribers pay a separate

fee to receive an individual program such as a sports event, movie, or concert.

PC *(noun)*
Abbreviation for personal computer.

peewee tech *(noun)*
Abbreviation for "peewee technology"—small companies in the telecommunications or computer-related industries. "Some think," observed *New York* magazine financial columnist Dan Dorfman in early 1985, that "peewee tech could be 1985's hottest stock group."

Peter Pan syndrome *(noun)*
Pop psychology term for the personality disorder that characterizes men who are emotionally childlike throughout their lives; title of a 1984 best-selling book.

petracide *(noun)*
The destruction of ancient historic stonework, as when bombs and artillery caused heavy damage to Ankor Wat in Cambodia during the Vietnam War or when, in 1985, terrorist bombs defaced Borobudur, a treasured Buddhist temple in Indonesia.

PG-13 *(adjective)*
A new movie-rating code created in 1984 by the Motion Picture Association of America. A straight PG rating on a film means that parental guidance is suggested because the film contains material that may be unsuitable for younger viewers; PG-13 signals parents to be especially cautious about sending children younger than thirteen to a movie so tagged. The new rating was prompted by strong criticism of the 1984 summer hits *Gremlins* and *Indiana Jones and the Temple of Doom*, both of which featured considerable gore.

phased array radar *(noun)*
An antiballistic-missile facility capable of locating multiple targets by omnidirectional scanning, tracking them simultaneously, and relaying data to other sites. American intelligence believes the Soviet Union to be building or operating at least six phased array radar systems.

photo opportunity *(noun)*
An occasion orchestrated to produce favorable and flattering photographs of the principals for the news media, especially in government and politics.

phreaking *(noun)*
Slang for the procedure by which *hackers* gain illegal use of telephone companies' long-distance services.

pick it *(verb)*
To field well, in baseball. A player who consistently makes good plays is said to be able to pick it, as in "Fred can really *pick it* at third."

PIN pin *or* pee-i-EN *(noun)*
Abbreviation for personal identification number. Telephone credit-card users, bank customers, and other consumers are assigned their own PINs, to be used for transactions with the issuing company.

pixel *(noun)*
Acronym for *pic*ture *el*ements. One of the tiny squares into which a photograph is broken down during computer photocompositing. Pixels can be manipulated along horizontal and vertical lines, enabling the operator to retouch or make composites or to alter the photograph in a way that cannot be detected in the finished picture.

plastic money *(noun)*
Credit and *debit cards*.

PMS *(noun)*
Abbreviation for premenstrual syndrome, a collection of symptoms displayed by some women prior to their periods of menstruation. Symptoms may include tension, irritability, and emotional volatility.

point guard *(noun)*
In basketball, the player charged with running the offense and, whenever possible, with handling the ball. The team's other guard, designated the off guard or shooting guard, is (often) a better shooter but a less adept ball handler.

poison pill defense *(noun)*
A device used to protect a corporation from an unwanted takeover. For example, a corporation can issue stock ("poison pill preferred," in Wall Street argot) to all its holders of common stock; by thus conferring special privileges on these stockholders, the corporation makes itself more expensive, or "poisonous" to swallow, for an outside raider.

policeman *(noun)*
In ice hockey, the player whose job is to protect his teammates or to punish, by fighting or hard checking, opponents who are harassing his teammates. This player is also called (by supporters of his opponents) a "goon" or an "enforcer."

pool reporter *(noun)*
One member of a large group of journalists who is selected to be present at a meeting or other event barred to the group as a whole. The pool reporter shares the information he gathers with his colleagues in return for the right to witness the event in question.

poop-scoop law *(noun)*
An ordinance requiring pet walkers to remove their pets' droppings from public areas. Poop-scoop laws, passed in a number of U.S. cities in the 1980s, resulted in the widespread use of the "pooper scooper," a device enabling the newly conscientious animal lovers to remain law-abiding.

PPI *(noun)*
Abbreviation for Producer Price Index. A system for estimating the future costs to consumers of manufactured goods by measuring industrial price changes.

prequel *(noun)*
A literary or cinematic work related to the story in an earlier work but written about events preceding those in the original. Edward I. Koch, for example, announced his plan to follow *Mayor*, his best-selling memoir about his years as New York City's chief executive, with a *prequel*—a book about his life before he entered politics.

progun *(adjective)*
Adhering to the presumed right of all citizens to bear arms; opposite of gun control. A progun candidate for office might be favored by such groups as the National Rifle Association or the John Birch Society.

PSI *(noun)*
Abbreviation for Pollution Standard Index, a system used by the U.S. Environmental Protection Agency (EPA) to measure the quality of the air. On a scale of 0 to 500, 0 to 50 is good, over 100 is unhealthy, and above 200 is hazardous. Los Angeles, for example, has ninety-five days a year that measure above PSI 200.

PT boat *(noun)*
In basketball, a small, quick guard.

puddle *(noun)*
A subsection of a company's inventory, usually containing only one of the product types included in the company's overall inventory, or "pool."

quality circle *(noun)*
A workers' committee in a factory that meets regularly to discuss problems in quality and production and to offer recommendations for improvement. A practice originating in Japan but increasingly popular with U.S. firms, which use it to boost employee morale and improve output and quality.

quartz-halogen lamp *(noun)*
An incandescent light fixture whose quartz bulb contains halogen gas and a tungsten filament; increasingly used for car headlights and other applications requiring brilliant illumination. The filament burns more intensely than those in ordinary bulbs and therefore produces a brighter and whiter light; the lamp also has a longer life than other bulbs, because the vaporized tungsten reacts with the halogen and is redeposited on the filament, constantly renewing it and preventing the blackening of the bulb.

Qube *(noun)*
Trademark for a two-way or *interactive cable* television system, first installed in Columbus, Ohio, in 1977 and expected to be extended to other areas. Qube, says *Advertising Age*, is "currently programmed locally with video tapes and offers movies, along with other programming, on a *pay-per-view* basis to about 270,000 subscribers in seven cities."

radial keratotomy *(noun)*
An operation, developed in the Soviet Union, to correct nearsightedness. A series of incisions are made radially in the cornea, changing the eye's shape and focal length.

radicchio ruh-DEE-kee-oh *(noun)*
A red-and-white-leafed chicory imported from Italy that gained sudden popularity with gourmet chefs in the mid-1980s. Vegetable importers reported that the demand for this pungent and colorful salad zoomed weekly sales in 1985 from one hundred pounds to twenty tons.

Radio Marti *(noun)*
A broadcasting service authorized by Congress to transmit a mix of daily radio programming, including propaganda, news, music, features, and sports, to Cuba. The service, named for the Cuban patriot and writer José Martí, was scheduled to begin broadcasting as a division of the Voice of America in 1985.

radon daughters *(noun)*
(See *passive smoking*.)

rainbow coalition *(noun)*
A group of people, usually connected by their support of a political candidate and composed of representatives of all races and economic levels. The phrase was used by the Reverend Jesse Jackson in his unsuccessful 1984 campaign for the Democratic presidential nomination; Jackson also called his coalition of black, Hispanic, American Indian, feminist, Arab-American, environmentalist, and Asian-American supporters a union of the "disenfranchised and ignored." The term was coined in 1982 by Texas Agriculture Commissioner Jim Hightower, who called his supporters "A rainbow coalition of blacks, browns, Anglos, blue-collar workers, and yellow-dog [unswervingly loyal] Democrats."

rain insurance *(noun)*
A policy issued by some underwriters to compensate vacationers for hotel and travel costs incurred during periods of rain or other inclement weather.

RAM ram *(noun)*
Acronym for reverse annuity mortgage. (See *reverse mortgage*.)

ranchera ron-CHAY-ruh *(noun)*
Spanish-style country and western music.

rapture *(verb)*
In fundamentalist Christian teaching, to carry the faithful to Jesus at the time of Armageddon, the battle between the forces of good and evil that will, fundamentalists believe, mark the end of the world. Signs inquiring, "Are you ready to be raptured?" appeared on city walls and lampposts with regularity in the mid-1980s.

Reaganaut *(noun)*
An ardent supporter of the policies of President Ronald Reagan. ("Reaganite" was an earlier term for such a supporter.)

rehaber REE-hab-ur *(noun)*
A member of one of several groups dedicated to wildlife preservation, who cares for injured or orphaned animals until the animals can be returned to the wild. There are two thousand licensed (by state and federal wildlife agencies) rehabers in the United States.

retrovirus *(noun)*
An unusual virus recently linked to three important diseases: cancer, acquired immunity deficiency syndrome (AIDS), and hepatitis. Its name comes from its possession of an enzyme that reverses the genetic information in normal cells.

reverse mortgage *(noun)*
Money borrowed in monthly installments from a lending institution that uses the borrower's house as collateral. Also known as an *IRMA* (individual retirement mortgage account) or a *RAM* (reverse annuity mortgage), a reverse mortgage is usually available only to people over the age of sixty; the borrower, in effect, puts up a small piece of his house each month for a guaranteed loan, which is not repayable unless the borrower sells the house. Otherwise, he continues to use the income and to live in his home, which will, on his death, be used to repay the loan.

revolving-door *(adjective)*
Phrase describing a policy or practice involving frequent changes in personnel, usually members of a company's administration.

right-to-die movement *(noun)*
A crusade whose principal tenet is that each individual has the legal and moral right to end his existence at a time of his own choosing.

riot shield *(noun)*
A resilient and lightweight screen carried by police officers or soldiers in self-defense against armed members of a hostile crowd.

roadie *(noun)*
A member of the technical support group that tours with a rock band.

robotronics *(noun)*
Popular toy robots that change into action figures or vehicles.

rock *(noun)*
A substance smoked by drug-users that is made by heating cocaine and wet baking soda. The fingernail-size "pebbles" that result from the process are sold for about twenty-five dollars each.

rock jock *(noun)*
A mountain-climbing enthusiast.

rocumentary *(noun)*
A feature-length theatrical movie whose principal content is a rock music concert or series of performances. Prince's *Purple Rain* and Talking Heads' *Stop Making Sense* are examples of the rocumentary, which is also known as the *movideo*—a contraction of "movie" and "video."

roll *(noun)*
A streak of good luck or high-performance ability. A team

with a string of victories, for example, or an author with several bestsellers in a row is said to be "on a roll."

rotator cuff *(noun)*
The four muscles and their tendons that reinforce the shoulder joint to give active support and still allow almost unlimited mobility. Damage to this system is a common sports injury, especially among baseball pitchers, who put great stress on it.

rubber-chicken *(adjective)*
Usually used to modify *circuit*; a round of banquets or political meetings characterized by interminable speeches and mass-produced, profoundly uninteresting, and overcooked food.

rumble strip *(noun)*
A portion of a highway studded with grooves or narrow sections of material that produce vibrations and a grating sound in the vehicles traveling over them; frequently employed by highway engineers to prevent motorists' drowsiness.

run-and-gun team *(noun)*
A basketball team whose principal strengths are fast running and accurate shooting ("gunning").

Ruppie RUP-ee *(noun)*
A word coined during the 1984 presidential campaign for "young urban Republican"; spinoff of *yuppie*.

Rustbelt *(noun)*
The Northeast and North-Central region of the United States containing the bulk of the nation's often deteriorating industrial cities.

sack *(noun)*
In football, the tackling of the quarterback by the defensive team behind the line of scrimmage.

Sagebrush Rebellion *(noun)*
A conservative political movement in the western United States advocating that millions of acres of federal land be turned over to state and private ownership. Members of the movement, which strongly supported Ronald Reagan in his 1980 and 1984 presidential campaigns, include former Interior Secretary James Watt and numerous ranchers, mine owners, timber executives, and power and gas company officials.

Sallie Mae *(noun)*
Popularly used name for the Student Loan Marketing Agency, which was chartered by Congress to free credit for student loans by buying loan portfolios and providing other financial services to banks and educational institutions.

Sandinistas *(noun)*
The popular name taken by members of Nicaragua's ruling Sandinist National Liberation Front (FSLN) from the revolutionary war hero General Augusto Cesar Sandino, who was assassinated in 1934 by the Nicaraguan National Guard.

sandwich music *(noun)*
A blend of jazz and rock music.

satellite antenna *(noun)*
A large, concave (or dish-shaped) receiver of broadcasting signals distributed by earth-orbiting satellites; used by consumers to bring in otherwise unobtainable television programs. By 1984, it was estimated that 600,000 satellite antennas adorned American backyards; 1985 was expected to bring that number to one million. A satellite antenna is also called a dish, downlink, or private earth station.

scientific creationism *(noun)*
The proposition of Christian fundamentalists that because "scientific" evidence supports the belief that God created life and the universe in its present form as described in the Bible, that belief should be taught in schools as a logical alternative to the Darwinian theory of evolution.

scorched earth *(noun)*
On the battlefield of corporate takeovers, a self-destructive strategy designed to make the target company less attractive to its assailants, perhaps by disposing of desirable assets or divisions or by arranging for all of its debts to come due at once in the event of a takeover.

script writer *(noun)*
A doctor who illegally sells prescriptions for painkillers, stimulants, and depressants for recreational use, some-

times operating under the cover of a "diet" or "stress" clinic.

scuzz *(noun)*
Anything or anyone distasteful, dirty, or contemptible. A scuzz can also be a *scuzzball*.

Seaspeak *(noun)*
A new, English-language, internationally used set of maritime terms that may, according to *U.S. News & World Report*, "become the official language of shipping."

secondhand smoke *(noun)*
(See *passive smoking*.)

shapesuit *(noun)*
A one-piece women's undergarment made of lightweight elastic material; not unlike what used to be called a *corset*, a word that, like *girdle*, has virtually disappeared from fashion's language.

shark repellent *(noun)*
Steps taken by a corporation to defend itself against a corporate raider, or "shark." "Among the most popular repellents in recent years," reported *Time* in 1985, "has been a requirement that a merger must be approved by at least 75 percent of the shareholders before it can take effect."

sidestream smoke *(noun)*
(See *passive smoking*.)

significant other *(noun)*
A boyfriend, girlfriend, or live-in lover; occasionally, a spouse.

SilverStone *(noun)*
Trademark for a chemically stable resin, similar to Teflon, which is applied to cooking utensils to prevent food from sticking to them.

sinsemilla sin-suh-MIL-uh *(noun)*
A seedless hybrid marijuana plant recently developed by American growers; reported by law enforcement officials to contain at least ten times as much of the narcotic THC as the Colombian variety, which was formerly considered the most potent of the cannabis family.

skell *(noun)*
A vagrant or other homeless person, usually one whose mental state ranges from eccentric to insane.

skotey *(noun)*
Acronym for "spoiled kid of the eighties." Skoteys, according to the *Wall Street Journal*, are the "baby boom kids of the baby boom." The paper reported in 1985 that a survey of this "class of [the year] 2000," numbers 10 million five-to-seven-year-olds and comprises 4.2 percent of the U.S. population.

slam dance *(noun)*
A type of punk-rock dance involving the energetic crashing of one pair of dancers into another pair.

slime *(verb)*
To wipe out in an unpleasant manner. Probably arising from the horror movies in which a gelatinous monster destroys its victim by oozing him to death. To *slime* is now commonly used along Madison Avenue: "How did they like your presentation?" "Negative. They slimed it." Also popularized by use in the film *Ghostbusters*, as in, "I've been slimed."

smart card *(noun)*
A plastic card developed in France that looks like an ordinary credit card but that contains a microprocessor capable of containing a file of bank balances, insurance records, financial records, or security codes for access to computer data bases.

smoke shop *(noun)*
A retail operation that sells marijuana and drug-use paraphernalia; also known as a head shop.

Solidarity *(noun)*
The outlawed Polish trade union led by Nobel Prize winner Lech Walensa.

sound bite *(noun)*
The short piece of video tape excerpted by television networks from their camera coverage of an event as significant or representative and shown repeatedly on newscasts. "The network sound bites indeed featured Reagan's lapses...." (*Newsweek*).

space telescope *(noun)*
An optical telescope to be put into orbit around the earth in 1985. Free of the effects of the atmosphere, it is expected to revolutionize astronomical observation.

spaghetti suit *(noun)*
Water-cooled long underwear worn by astronauts. The water is circulated through hundreds of feet of mini-tubing woven into the fabric.

Spanglish *(noun)*
An urban patois composed of words and word-part combinations (such as *Nuevo York*) drawn from Spanish and English.

Spetsnaz SPET-snahz *(noun)*
Russian word for Soviet special forces units trained by the KGB to attack military sites at the onset of any major East-West conflict.

spin control *(noun)*
The effort of a press agent or public relations expert to impart a favorable slant, or *spin*, to a news story relating to a client. Such a practitioner is a *spin doctor*.

spreadsheet *(noun)*
A computer program that displays columns into which the user inserts figures; the program recomputes all relevant totals and percentages with each added or deleted figure.

squeal rule *(noun)*
The controversial 1983 decision made by the Department of Health, Education, and Welfare that doctors must report the requests of minors for contraception to their parents.

squeeze *(noun)*
Girlfriend or boyfriend.

starch blocker *(noun)*
A patent medicine claimed by its manufacturers to be able to prevent the body from digesting the starch and carbohydrates in food; termed dangerous by the Food and Drug Administration because it causes serious digestive problems.

Star Wars defense *(noun)*
Popular name for the high-tech missile defense system proposed by President Reagan and known to his administration as the Strategic Defense Initiative. The system would theoretically provide a defensive shield against hostile missiles, thus eliminating the need for the strategic

doctrine of mutually assured destruction (MAD) now prevailing.

stealth bomber *(noun)*
A military aircraft under development by the United States; featuring advanced technology and a slim profile, it is designed to be invisible to enemy radar.

stevioside STEE-vee-oh-syd *(noun)*
A naturally occurring, low-calorie sweetener from the plant *stevia*; much sweeter than sugar but without the aftertaste of saccharin.

stick it *(verb)*
To land on one's feet—literally or figuratively—solidly and effortlessly. The phrase comes from the world of gymnastics, where it means to return to the mat after a flip as though there were a spike extending from the bottom of each foot; thus, to land without wavering. "How was your first day on the job?" "Great. I stuck it."

sunblock *(noun)*
An ointment or cream containing agents that prevent the tanning rays of the sun from getting through to the skin.

sunchoke *(noun)*
The tuber of the Jerusalem artichoke, an edible vegetable.

superfund *(noun)*
Money designated by Congress to finance the cleanup of *toxic waste*.

superstation *(noun)*
A conventional TV station whose programming is made available via satellite to cable systems across the country. Atlanta's WTBS became America's first superstation in 1976.

supertitle *(noun)*
In opera, the simultaneous translation of the libretto on a screen above the stage; an innovation seen by Beverly Sills, director of the New York City Opera, as a way to break down the communication gap between opera and audience. Also called *surtitle*; derived from *subtitle*.

surrogate mother *(noun)*
1. A female who gives birth to an offspring as the result of the surgical implantation of an embryo conceived by another female. 2. A woman who gives birth to an artificially inseminated child that she has agreed, usually for a stipulated payment, to carry for and relinquish to an infertile woman.

sweeps *(noun)*
The months set by the Nielson and Arbitron ratings services—November, February, and May—to establish the ranking of the television network shows, which determines the advertising rates for local stations.

sysop SIS-op *(noun)*
(See *bulletin-board system*.)

tablescape *(noun)*
A scene created by the placement of decorative objects, books, photographs, etc., on a surface such as a bookcase, piano, shelf, or table; used primarily in interior decorating.

table setters *(noun)*
In baseball, the first two hitters of the lineup, whose job it is to get on base ("set the table") for the sluggers who follow them.

talking head *(noun)*
1. In television commercials, a shot of an individual persuasively explaining the qualities of a product. 2. To a filmmaker, "talking heads" means footage of two actors in conversation, with no other action.

tapas TOP-uhs *(noun)*
An increasingly popular form of hors d'oevres, originally served in bars and restaurants in Spain. A typical *tapas* may include clams in garlic sauce, strips of fried squid or thin, skewered slices of ham or cheese. From the Spanish

tapa, which means "lid," and applied to this menu item because it was originally served covering a bottle or small glass of wine or beer. "Today," writes food critic Montse Guillen, "the variety of *tapas* is so diverse that many international diners compare it to the ritual of Chinese *dim sum*, and, as in that Chinese banquet, the key is to sample small quantities of many dishes."

tapped out *(adjective)*
Without money; drained of financial resources.

techie TEK-ee *(noun)*
Abbreviation of technician. Someone who is both expert at and dedicated to the creation, development, and use of sophisticated equipment, particularly computers.

Teflon *(adjective)*
The property, named for the trademarked antistick resin used on cooking utensils, that enables its possessor to shed with ease the effects of bad times and get credit for good; commonly applied to President Reagan's immunity from all the traditional laws of politics, as in "the Teflon factor" (*Newsweek*) or "the Teflon presidency" (Washington *Post*).

telecommuter *(noun)*
An individual who works at home and "commutes" to an office via a computer or telephone lines instead of by car or train. American telecommuters—whose number, the *Wall Street Journal* reports, could exceed 7.2 million by the end of 1985—are frequently employed as computer programmers, systems analysts, software developers, writers, researchers, and consultants. The *Journal* also notes that IBM has installed more than eight thousand computers in employees' homes, thereby enabling them to work overtime away from the office. (See also *electronic cottage*.)

Tex-Mex *(adjective)*
Relating to Mexican cooking with an American influence.

the whole nine yards *(noun)*
Everything connected with a given object or process. "The town's newest playpen is 'The Drinkery,' a palace of preposterous trendiness that features expensive drinks, stained glass, exposed brick, hanging plants—the whole nine yards" (Saybrook *Gazette*). (The phrase originated as praise for a tailor; when a patron bought the nine yards of fabric required for a suit, and the tailor, not scrimping, used all of it, he was commended for giving "the whole nine yards.")

Tofutti tuh-FOO-tee *(noun)*
The trademarked name for tofu "ice cream," invented by Brooklyn entrepreneur David Mintz as a dairy-free dessert for consumers who keep kosher and cannot eat meat and dairy food at the same meal, and as a viable dessert alternative for people on low-cholesterol or low-lactose diets.

toxic waste *(noun)*
The hazardous by-products of chemical and manufacturing industries. Methods for the disposing of toxic waste, because it is a threat to health and the environment, are a volatile political subject in the United States.

toyetic *(adjective)*
Having the potential for being translated into a popular toy, as, for example, the TV character "The Six-Million-Dollar Man" or the characters from the film *Star Wars*.

TR *(noun)*
Abbreviation for treasury receipt, a type of *zero*.

tradecraft *(noun)*
Term used in espionage for the body of knowledge and

skills necessary for an intelligence agent to operate successfully undercover.

transdermal *(adjective)*
Literally, "through the skin." The transdermal patch, developed as a safe, effective, and easy way to administer drugs, is a medicated adhesive strip from which a drug is absorbed into the skin in a steady dosage over a period of time.

transition game *(noun)*
The point in a basketball game at which the two sides switch, respectively, from offense to defense; a key buzzword in 1980s basketball. Teams adept at the transition game are usually well supplied with *greyhounds* and are generally characterized as *run-and-gun teams*; teams less adept at the transition game are likely to be stocked with "plodders"—big, slow players—and prefer to play a "half-court" game (to be slow in setting up their offense).

trash-to-energy system *(noun)*
An electric power plant fueled with trash or garbage, burned at extremely high temperatures. The intense heat is said to destroy odors and pollutants and, not incidentally, to destroy the trash. In increasing use in such cities as Boston, which has a trash-to-energy system that consumes twelve hundred tons of refuse per day.

triathlon *(noun)*
An athletic competition that usually includes, in order, a 1½-mile swim, a 25-mile bicycle ride, and a 10-mile run. A participant in a triathlon is a triathlete.

triathatards try-ATH-uh-tardz *(ath* as in *bath) (noun)*
One-piece, space-age fabric exercise costume that hugs the body from neck to ankle. Similar to leotards, triathatards,

which take their name from the newly popular form of athletics, are also known as "skinsuits."

Trivial Pursuit *(noun)*
The trademarked name for a popular board game based on questions and answers about trivia from historical and contemporary culture.

tropicalism *(noun)*
The synthesis of elements from jazz, rock, and Caribbean music with traditional and popular Brazilian music.

Unimog YOO-nuh-mog *(noun)*
A street-cleaning device coming into use in U.S. cities. The machine, sometimes called a "super truck," is said to be capable of vacuuming between parked cars, plowing or inhaling snow, spreading salt, and compacting trash. "It looks," reported *The New York Times*, "like the offspring of a garbage truck mated with a vacuum cleaner, and it emits an unearthly, ear-shattering noise."

user-friendly *(adjective)*
Easy to use. *User-friendly* was originally applied to computers designed for simplified operation, but the word has come to mean "accessible" or "easily understood" and is used to describe anything from a textbook to a kitchen appliance. "The headquarters of *USA Today* is handsomely decorated with the same user-friendly efficiency that is built into computers" (*Time*). (When *The New York Times* made a reference to a new line of chocolate candy made in the shape of computer disks—by a company called Sweetware, Inc.—it headlined the item "Eater-Friendly.")

vaporization *(noun)*
The transformation of all living and inanimate matter into mist; often used to refer to the hypothetical aftermath of a nuclear war.

video *(noun)*
A brief (three- to ten-minute) film clip, usually made for television, that uses a popular record as the soundtrack for a minifilm. Most videos are made with rock music, hence, rock video; a popular showcase for the form is the cable network *MTV*.

video club *(noun)*
A lounge or cafe where the entertainment consists of *videos* shown on numerous television screens.

video jock *(noun)*
A master of ceremonies or announcer for a television program or *video club*. Sometimes called a VJ.

Walkman *(noun)*
Trademark for a small, portable tape playback device with lightweight earphones.

walk-on *(noun)*
An athlete "auditioning" for a place on a college team who was not specifically recruited to play.

wave *(noun)*
A fad among fans at sports events in which audience members rise sequentially, raise their arms, wave their hands, and scream rhythmically. "... The wave looks like one of those monster trends" (J.McGrath, Denver *Post*).

wax *(verb)*
To defeat. "The people have not seen us waxed like this in three years," said Knicks spokesman Hubie Brown after a particularly humiliating loss. Political columnists Rowland Evans and Robert Novak wrote about a Reagan strategist who was "ecstatic over the waxing of Walter Mondale."

wedge buster (noun)
In football, a player whose job it is to break up the opposing team's array of blockers ("wedge") on kickoffs, usually by hurling himself at high speed into as many of the opponents as possible. This player is sometimes also called a "kamikaze."

white knight (noun)
A corporation that rescues another corporation from a raider in a takeover battle. The white knight acquires the threatened firm on more favorable terms than the raider would provide; such terms might include a higher price for the acquired firm's stock and a guarantee that its executives will be retained.

window (noun)
Almost any opening in almost anything. To a NASA technician, a window is the time period in which a rocket can be successfully launched into a specific path; to a rush-hour commuter, it is the portion of the train schedule that falls between the heaviest traffic patterns; to a computer operator, it is one of several programs that can be simultaneously viewed on a single screen; to the military, a "window of vulnerability" is the defense gap that could be filled with the enemy's weapons.

wired (adjective)
In a state of feverish agitation, usually due to drugs, such as cocaine.

wonk (noun)
Bookworm. "Wonk," noted a 1985 *New York Times* editorial, "means grind, and an unattractive one at that, sporting a plastic nerd pack for pens and wearing glasses repaired with adhesive tape. To be called, by comparison, an *airhead* is almost a compliment."

worst-case scenario *(noun)*
A projection of the direst possible outcome of a hypothetical sequence of events; also, a course of action to deal with such an outcome.

wound laboratory *(noun)*
The Defense Department's firing range on the campus of the national military medical school in Bethesda, Maryland, where animals are shot with high-powered weapons so their wounds can be studied by surgeons and scientists. Revelation of the wound lab's existence, with which the government trains doctors in battlefield medicine, created a widespread public outcry, especially from members of the *animal rights movement*.

yellow rain *(noun)*

A yellow, clinging mist first reported in Southeast Asia in the 1970s; said to cause nausea, bleeding, and sometimes death. First suspected of being an instrument of chemical warfare, with resulting international recriminations. Subsequent scientific investigation, however, suggests that it is a natural phenomenon, possibly bee excrement containing a toxin-producing fungus.

yumpie *(noun)*

Acronym for a young, upwardly mobile professional, a close relative of the slightly earlier *yuppie*, a young urban professional. Both words became popular in the early 1980s as the advertising and sales sectors of the economy recognized the almost limitless purchasing power represented by these trendy, ambitious city dwellers, all of whom were *baby boomers*. Newsweek called yuppies "a generation focused on careers, condos, and the latest cuisines," and added, "Yuppies are proving they can have it all; they've reclaimed the old neighborhoods, climbed the corporate ladders and built perfect bodies." *Yuppie* appears frequently in such merchandising efforts as that of the Ford Motor Company for its Aerostar *minivan*, a vehicle Ford calls a "yuppiemobile."

yup-com *(noun)*
A television show aimed at *yuppies*. The word is a spinoff from sit-com, the half-hour comedy-plot shows that began to occupy prime-time television in the 1950s. A yup-com, according to Peter W. Kaplan in *The New York Times*, is "a continuing story about people in the demographic group the network hopes will identify with its product: 18 to 49 years old, upwardly mobile, urban professionals, often single."

yuppie *(noun)*
(See *yumpie.*)

zap *(verb)*
To eliminate television commercials by using the fast-for-ward control on a videocassette recorder; some viewers also practice zapping by using a remote-control device to shut off the audio portion of the transmission during com-mercials. A Nielson study, reported in *Advertising Age*, "showed that 64 percent of those viewers who tape shows zap the commercials."

ZapMail *(noun)*
Trade name used by the Federal Express Corporation for an electronic mail service capable of transmitting copies of correspondence across the United States in two hours or less.

zero *(noun)*
Short form for zero coupon bond, a long-term U.S. Treas-ury security whose coupons are removed and sold sepa-rately from the bond itself. Instead of carrying coupons to be clipped for the payment of interest every six months, zeros are sold at a fraction of their face value; when they

mature—in ten to twenty years—their holders receive a single payment that includes all accrued interest.

zero option *(noun)*
An arms control proposal calling for the United States and the Soviet Union to withdraw all missiles from Europe.

Zip + 4 Code *(noun)*
The Postal Service's new, nine-digit zip code system for first-class mail, which, the service asserts, will provide speedier and cheaper mailing for corporations and educational institutions. (The Zip + 4 Code for the U.S. Postal Service in Washington, D.C., is 20013-2999.)

zoo plane *(noun)*
(See *animal*.)

zydeco ZY-dik-oh *(noun)*
Cajun dance music, originally from southern Louisiana but recently popular in urban areas, that has French-dialect lyrics and syncopated rhythms played on the piano, accordion, guitar, and *frottoir* (rub-board).

INDEX

ABBREVIATIONS AND ACRONYMS

THE ARTS; ENTERTAINMENT

ambisonic
breakdancing
chatcom
compact disk
cruciverbalist
dancercise
electric boogie
electrofunk
ghetto blaster
gorilla
hip-hop
Jazzercise
Klezmer music
legs
lockbox
maximinimalism
mego
moonwalk
movideo
MTV
pay-per-view

PG-13
prequel
Qube
Radio Marti
ranchera
roadie
rocumentary
sandwich music
satellite antenna
slam dance
sound bite
superstation
toyetic
Trivial Pursuit
tropicalism
video
video club
video jock
Walkman
yup-com
zydeco

BUSINESS AND FINANCE

bargaining chip
big-ticket
cash cow
CEO
circuit breaker
critical path
debit card
ECU
EOE
factory farming
Fannie Mae
first-sale doctrine
focus group
Fortune 500
Freddie Mac
Ginnie Mae
golden handcuffs
golden handshake
gorilla
gray market
greenmail
greenshoe

grumpie
hypermarket
insider trading
IRMA
job shop
junk bond
just-in-time
kanban
Laffer curve
LBO
lemon law
line extension
liquidity trap
misery index
MMDA
minivan
outsourcing
Pac-man maneuver
peewee tech
PIN
plastic money
poison pill defense

PPI
PSI
puddle
RAM
reverse mortgage
Sallie Mae
scorched earth
shark repellent

smart card
sweeps
tapped out
telecommuter
TR
white knight
ZapMail
zero

COMPUTERS

Arkie
artificial intelligence
BBS
bulletin-board system
CAD/CAM
CAE
chip revolution
computer commuter
computer hedgehog
computerist
computer monitoring
cracker
electronic cottage
electronic mail
fifth-generation computer
hacker

intelligent
log off
mail merging
mechatronics
menu
optical processor
PC
peewee tech
phreaking
pixel
spreadsheet
sysop
techie
telecommuter
user-friendly

CRIMINAL AND LEGAL

CAMP
checkbook witness
chop shop
coyote
deep pocket
devastator bullet
first-sale doctrine
flutter
goonda
Guardian Angels

insider trading
lemon law
marital rape
poop-scoop law
riot shield
rock
script writer
sinsemilla
smoke shop

ENVIRONMENT

afterburst
bubble concept
no-till
nuclear waste
nuclear winter
omnicide
petracide

PSI
Rustbelt
superfund
toxic waste
trash-to-energy system
Unimog
vaporization
yellow rain

FOOD AND DRINK

aristology
blackened fish
Cajun popcorn
Cavaillon
dirty rice
gravlaks
grazing
nopalitos

radicchio
SilverStone
starch blocker
stevioside
sunchoke
tapas
Tex-Mex
Tofutti

HEALTH AND MEDICINE

acyclovir
aging gene
Ames test
bonding
box
B-strep
chlamydia
cosmoceutical
cryobirth
ETS
gateway drug
gene therapy
gomer
Jarvik 7
Marfan syndrome
medigap
MicroTrak
minoxidil

oncogene
opportunistic infection
passive smoking
PMS
radial keratotomy
radon daughters
retrovirus
rotator cuff
script writer
sidestream smoke
squeal rule
starch blocker
sunblock
surrogate mother
transdermal
wired
wound laboratory
yellow rain

INTERNATIONAL AFFAIRS

Anzus
black spot
boatlift
Contadora
contra
Cosmograd
coyote
ECU
English creep
Euromissile
evil empire
Gang of Four
global village
golpe

Great Leap Forward
Greens
Helsinki Agreement
la langue du Coca-Cola
liberation theology
nomenklatura
phased array radar
Radio Marti
Seaspeak
Solidarity
Spetsnaz
tradecraft
yellow rain
zero option

LANGUAGE

airhead
allophone
animal
baby boomer
blow off
box
busters
camel
cattle show
chicken hawk
coyote
deep pocket
dorky
English creep
fuzzword
Gang of Four
gomer
gorilla
granola
grazing
Great Leap Forward
grumpie

hat trick
hip-hop
human resources
key
la langue du Coca-Cola
legs
loopy
misery index
motormouth
muppie
net-net
nose candy
peewee tech
Peter Pan syndrome
phreaking
Reaganaut
roll
rubber chicken
scorched earth
scuzz
Seaspeak
shark repellent

skell
slime
Spanglish
squeeze
stick it
tapped out
techie
Teflon

the whole nine yards
user-friendly
wax
white knight
window
worst-case scenario
wonk

LIFESTYLE

aristology
aromatherapy
baby boomer
bareboat
bicoastal
birth parent
camcorder
cosmoceutical
cross-dressing
dancercise
deep pocket
downscale
English creep
ETS
Flashing
flutter
401 (k) Plan
fourth degree
gateway drug
gender gap
ghetto blaster
gîte
Gore-Tex

granola
gray market
grazing
Greens
Guardian Angels
hair extension
high-five
hip-hop
hypermarket
Jazzercise
Kevlar
lockbox
male bonding
me generation
midlife crisis
minivan
muppie
passive smoking
Peter Pan syndrome
PG-13
plastic money
Qube
roadie

rock
rock jock
rubber chicken
shapesuit
sidestream smoke
significant other
skell
skotey
smart card
Spanglish
squeal rule
squeeze
stick it
surrogate mother

tablescape
telecommuter
triathatards
Trivial Pursuit
video club
video jock
Walkman
wave
yumpie
yup-com
yuppie
zap
zydeco

MANAGEMENT AND ORGANIZATION

bargaining chip
cafeteria plan
computer monitoring
critical path
EOE
flutter
401 (k) Plan
fourth degree
golden handcuffs

golden handshake
human resources
just-in-time
kanban
micromanagement
outsourcing
quality circle
revolving door

THE MEDIA

advertorial
animal
busters
checkbook journalism
chilling effect
communications satellite
community channels
DBS
footprint
geostationary satellite
infomercial
interactive cable
mail merging
mediagenic

pay-per-view
PG-13
photo opportunity
pool reporter
prequel
Qube
sound bite
spin control
superstation
sweeps
talking head
video
yup-com
zap

THE MILITARY

Ada
afterburst
Anzus
build-down
defcon
dense pack
first strike
football
Hummer

light infantry
micromanagement
mini-RPV
phased array radar
Spetsnaz
Star Wars defense
stealth bomber
wound laboratory
zero option

MOVEMENTS AND CAUSES

animal rights movement
antichoice
antilifer
freezenik
Greens
liberation theology
me generation

progun
rainbow coalition
rapture
rehaber
right-to-die movement
Sagebrush Rebellion
scientific creationism

PRODUCTS AND SERVICES

aromatherapy
ATM
bonding
camcorder
cellular phone
CEO
compact disk
cooler
debit card
Dungeons and Dragons
electronic mail
ergometer
Flashing
Gore-Tex
hair extension
Hummer
hypermarket
job shop
Kevlar
LA
line extension
minivan
mousse
MTSO

PIN
plastic money
quartz-halogen lamp
rain insurance
RAM
reverse mortgage
robotronics
rumble strip
satellite antenna
shapesuit
SilverStone
smart card
space telescope
spaghetti suit
stealth bomber
sunblock
Tofutti
transdermal
trash-to-energy system
Trivial Pursuit
Unimog
Walkman
ZapMail
Zip + 4 Code

POLITICS

animal
Atari Democrat
barn burner
black spot
cattle show
evil empire
exit poll
gender gap
Greens
item veto

neocon
neoliberal
photo opportunity
rainbow coalition
Reaganaut
Ruppie
Sagebrush Rebellion
superfund
Teflon
zoo plane

SPORTS

aircraft carrier
bump and run
cross-training
ergometer
gamer
greyhound
head hunter
high-five
monster man
pick it
point guard
policeman
PT boat

rock jock
roll
rotator cuff
run-and-gun team
sack
stick it
table setters
transition game
triathlon
triathatards
wave
wedge buster

SPACE, SCIENCE, AND NATURE

aging gene
agrigenetics
Bambi syndrome
biobelt
bioreactor
bubble concept
caramel
chip revolution
Cosmograd
cryobirth
cryptozoology
DBS
dustman
facedness

fast burn
gene therapy
geostationary satellite
Jarvik 7
mechatronics
mousse
no-till
nuclear waste
nuclear winter
omnicide
satellite antenna
space telescope
spaghetti suit
vaporization

Do you have any appropriate new words, additions or suggestions for our next edition of the NEW WORDS DICTIONARY? If so, send them to:

Sid Lerner
c/o Ballantine Books
201 East 50th Street
New York, New York 10022

Remember, no compensation or credit can be given, and only appropriate suggestions will be included.

ABOUT THE AUTHORS

HAROLD LeMAY is a lifelong linguist, painter, and sculptor. Since he graduated from Boston University, he has worked at a variety of jobs—including a seventeen-year stint at Monsanto—adding constantly to his two-thousand-volume personal library and extensive vocabulary. He is currently studying fine art at the Lyme Academy in Old Lyme, Connecticut.

SID LERNER is a book packager and new products developer with a background in advertising and a nose for trends.

MARIAN TAYLOR is the head of her own editing service and has worked on projects for Reader's Digest Books, Chelsea House Publishers, and Collier's Encyclopedia. Prior to that, she worked for *The New York Times* Syndicate, *The Los Angeles Times* Syndicate, and *Life*.